LARRY LI

LEARN GUITAR BOOK

VOLUME 1

SPECIAL THANKS TO:
RC LITTLE, JACK and HANK KALVIN
Editors: Mathew Dalessi and Larry Little
Graphic Design: CDS Graphics, Glendale, CA and Larry Little
Photography: Phi Vu

BY LARRY LITTLE

ISBN 1-884208-08-8

THE LARRY LITTLE COMPANY
P. O. BOX 413005 SUITE#101
NAPLES, FLORIDA 33941-3005

FORWARD

The information contained in this book is distilled from many years of teaching expertise. It is my intention to pass on this information as it has been successfully used with positive results for over 25 years with thousands of students. From time to time, teaching professionals differ in their approach as to what works for them in their practices. Years of professional experience have taught me to work with, and encourage, each individual student as to what works for him or her in the interest of the most positive results in the shortest length of time. The goal of this book is to cover the basics of learning guitar from a popular music standpoint, not from a schooled, disciplined approach. The idea is to have fun with the instrument. I certainly encourage private instruction whenever possible. Any knowledge gained in the pursuit of learning the instrument can only be helpful.

– Larry Little

INTRODUCTION

Larry Little's "Learn Guitar Book" volume 1 can be used as a stand alone learning, practice, and study guide or with the video "Learn Guitar on VCR" volume 1. The numbers on the bottom corners of each page provide a reference guide to help you coordinate the use of the book with the video tape. By using the fast forward or reverse on your tape machine you can locate and review sections of the video tape that correspond with the book. You can also use the digital counter found on most vcr machines. To do this reset your vcr counter at the beginning of the tape where the video clock first appears. Then as you play through the tape, take note of the different sections you want to review by writing down the counter numbers in the blank space provided next to the video clock numbers listed in the book. The exercise chord progressions correspond with the songs found in the "video songbook" section of LARRY LITTLE'S "Learn Guitar on VCR" volume 1 video. Now let's "LEARN GUITAR".

TABLE OF CONTENTS

TABLE OF CONTENTS

GENERAL GUITAR AND PLAYING INFORMATION

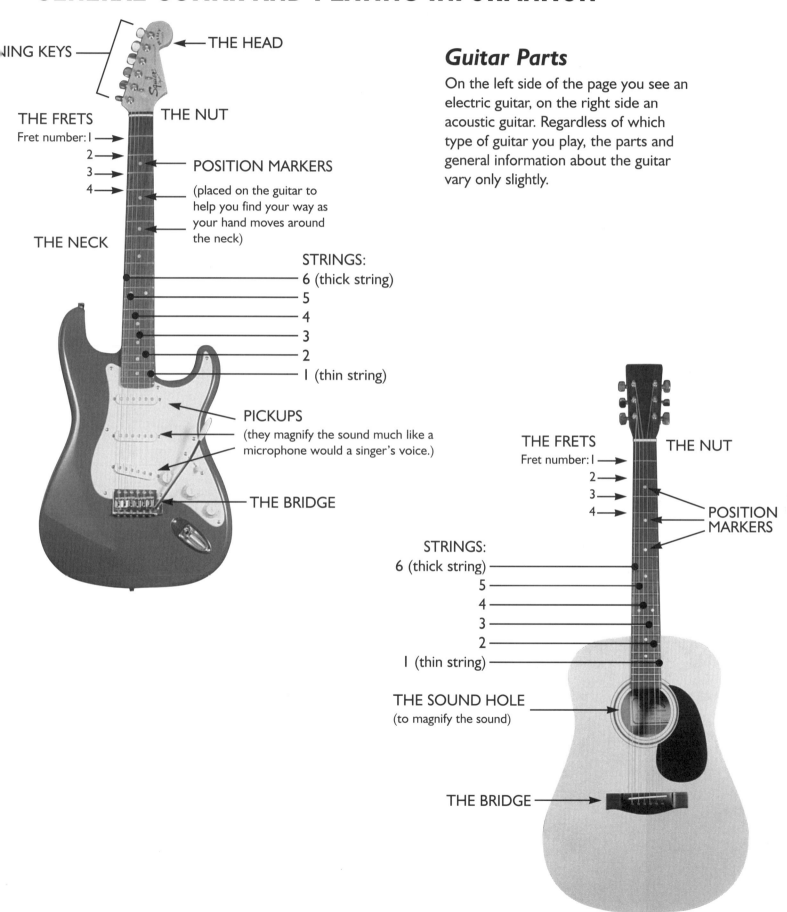

NING KEYS — ← THE HEAD

THE FRETS
Fret number: 1 →
2 →
3 →
4 →

THE NUT

POSITION MARKERS

(placed on the guitar to help you find your way as your hand moves around the neck)

THE NECK

STRINGS:
6 (thick string)
5
4
3
2
1 (thin string)

PICKUPS
(they magnify the sound much like a microphone would a singer's voice.)

THE BRIDGE

Guitar Parts

On the left side of the page you see an electric guitar, on the right side an acoustic guitar. Regardless of which type of guitar you play, the parts and general information about the guitar vary only slightly.

THE FRETS
Fret number: 1 →
2 →
3 →
4 →

THE NUT

POSITION MARKERS

STRINGS:
6 (thick string)
5
4
3
2
1 (thin string)

THE SOUND HOLE
(to magnify the sound)

THE BRIDGE

1:15

Sitting and Standing Positions to Play Guitar

Standing position to play guitar

Sitting Position to play guitar

Sequence in Proper Holding of the Instrument

Hold the guitar on your right leg.

Sit on a firm upright chair.
Try and keep the guitar tucked in
close to the body.

It's best to keep your guitar up close
to your body and turn your head to
see the guitar's neck.

*Note: If you are right handed you will be strumming and picking out notes with the right hand.
Your left hand will be holding and fingering the neck of the guitar. It is common for some left handed
people to play right handed. However some choose to restring their guitars to play left handed.*

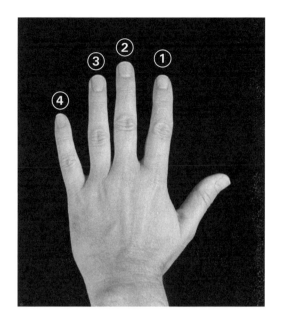

The Left Hand Fingers

The fingers you use to pick out notes and hold chords.
When playing guitar, you don't count the thumb as one of your fingers.

All About Picks

Guitar picks usually come in different thicknesses: thin, medium, heavy, and extra heavy. Although you may want to use your thumb to strum or fingers to pick out notes, I suggest you use a pick at first to help you develop a good rhythm style. Later as you progress you'll want to try other styles of playing including finger picking with the right hand. As you continue to play, you'll discover all kinds of picks. Experiment with them until you find the type, size, and thickness you prefer.

Proper Picking

Hold the pick between your thumb and first finger. Hold it firmly, but not too tightly. If there is a point to the pick, it should be facing toward the strings. This is the most common way to hold the pick. If you have a pick, strum the guitar without touching or fingering any strings on the neck. If you don't have a pick, strum with your thumb. The first thing you'll notice is that your guitar may not sound right. It may be out of tune.

⏱ 2:34

HOW TO TUNE YOUR GUITAR

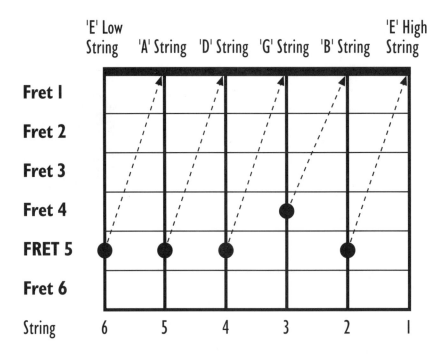

There are different ways to tune your guitar and different devices that you can use to help you tune. Above you see a standard diagram that shows you how to tune your guitar by ear. Your 6th string or the thickest string should be tuned to a low "E" pitch or sound. Without a piano, or one of the devices described later in this section it is difficult to establish the "E" pitch of your 6th string. However you can still tune your guitar by using the chart above. Place your finger on the 6th string at the 5th fret. (Place your finger just behind the 5th fret bar for the best sound.) Pick that note, followed by picking out the 5th string open (no finger on the fretboard). The two strings should match in sound. If they don't, your 5th string is out of tune. Carefully turn the 5th string tuning peg till the sound of the 5th string matches the sound of the 6th string held down at the 5th fret. Follow the diagram above and do the same for each string until you get to the 2nd string. To tune the 2nd string, place your finger on the 3rd string, 4th fret. Now pick the 3rd and the 2nd strings out and get them to match. After you've tuned the 2nd string, go back to the 2nd string, 5th fret. Now pick the 2nd and the 1st strings out until they match. Tuning by ear is important, but at first it can be difficult. There are other products that can help you tune your guitar.

Tuning Fork

This is used to help you establish the original pitch to which you tune.

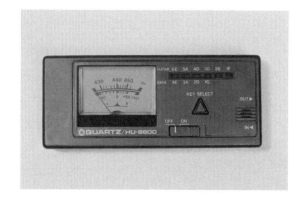

Pitchpipe

This helps you establish the pitch of each individual string. Try to match as closely as possible the sound of each one of your guitar strings to the tone you hear. A piano or keyboard can also help you accomplish this.

Electronic Guitar Tuner

This is a guitar tuner which will greatly simplify tuning your guitar. I would highly recommend one of these. With a guitar tuner you play the string you want to tune, and the device tells you when you're in pitch range, and finally in tune. After you've finished tuning your guitar strum it down slowly from ceiling to floor and listen carefully. If it's in tune it should sound even and melodic.

OPENING SINGLE NOTE EXERCISE

Warm-up exercise #1

This exercise will help you coordinate your right hand with your left. During the exercise pick the first note down, the next note up, and the next down. Always alternate your picking. This enables you to play faster, smoother, and with a more even stroke. You don't have to hold all the strings down at the same time.

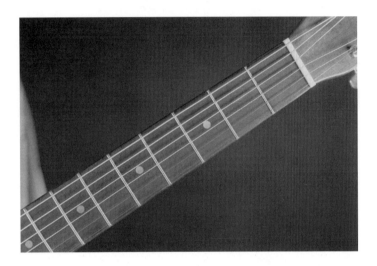

Starting with a down stroke, the symbol for which is "ⁿ", pick the 6th string open (no fingers of your left hand on the fretboard).

Next, place your 1st finger (your index finger) on string 6, fret 1. The idea is to play as close to the fret bar as possible for a clean sound. Don't play on the fret bar, play just behind it, in the fret you want to play.

Now place your 2nd finger on string 6, fret 2.

Next string 6, fret 3.

String 6, finger on fret 4.

So you play open,1,2,3,4 on the 6th string. Now pick out each individual string just like you did on the 6th string starting on the 5th string open(no fingers), followed by string 5, fret 1. String 5, fret 2. String 5, fret 3. String 5, fret 4. So you play open 1,2,3,4 on the 5th string. Repeat the same for each string open 1,2,3,4 until you finish on string 1, fret 4. Now from that same note play backwards 4,3,2,1 open on the 1st string. Play 4,3,2,1 open on the 2nd string. 4,3,2,1 open on the 3rd string. 4,3,2,1 open on the 4th string. 4,3,2,1 open on the 5th string, and finally 4,3,2,1 open on the 6th string.

*Note: *It is very important, right from the beginning that you use a down-up stroke (n-down stroke, v-up stroke) when you're picking single string notes.*

*Note: *Practice slowly and evenly paced. Build your speed. Listen for the quality of each note.*

*Note: *Pat your foot as you play. Keep a slow and steady deliberate beat 1,2,3,4. Pick one note to each beat.*

TABLATURE SYSTEMS

There are different systems for writing out notes and melody line in guitar music. Standard musical notation is used as well as different types of what is called guitar "tablature". One type of tablature notates the specific string and fret to play. The first number is the string, followed by the fret you play it on. For example:

String/Fret: 6/0 6/1 6/2 6/3
(string six, fret open)(string six, fret one) etc...

This is called "string/fret" tablature. You listen to the sound source "recording" and play along. This tablature system is a general guide to help you use and develop your listening skills. This is called "playing by ear".

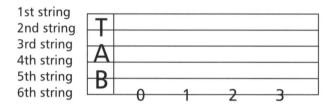

Above you see another kind of tablature system which involves a diagram of the six strings of the guitar with numbers that represent the frets. This method is perhaps more effective in helping you find the particular notes to play. However we will be using the first system of tablature to help you in "maximum ear development". This system is used in the video LARRY LITTLE'S "Learn Guitar on VCR" volume 1 and volume 2.

Warm-up exercise #1 was a single string or solo note exercise in which you picked out one note at a time. Next, we'll learn about chords. Chords are a group of notes played on the guitar all at once. Unlike single notes, you strum, strike, stroke, pick or pluck out chords. These particular chords have been chosen in order of their progressive difficulty and musicality. I recommend that you learn them in this order.

CHORD EXERCISES AND STRUM PATTERNS

The Chord Diagram

Guitar with chord diagram overlay
(as you would face the guitar)

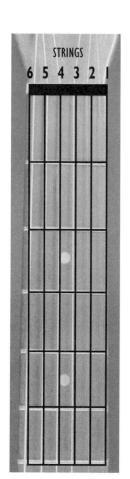

Guitar with chord diagram overlay (guitar turned vertically)

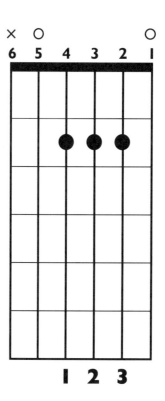

The Standard Chord Diagram

To the right is a chord diagram. It is actually a graphic representation of the guitar's neck and fretboard. This is the standard you'll find in most guitar music for the chord diagrams of where to place your fingers on the fretboard. The frets are drawn horizontally. The strings run vertically. The numbers at the top of the diagram are the string numbers 6,5,4,3,2, and1. The "x" above the string number means you don't play that particular string. The "o" above the string number means that the particular string is played 'open' (with no fingers on any fret). The numbers below the diagram are the fingers to use to hold the chord.

7:36

The "A" Major Chord

A

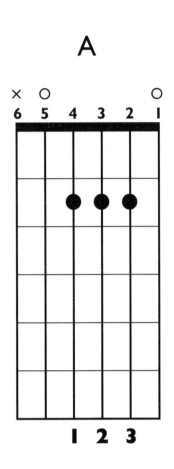

To read a chord using the diagram the fingers are placed on the diagram as dots. This is a picture of the first chord you are going to learn. It is called the "A" or "A" major chord. The numbers at the top are the strings of the guitar. The numbers at the bottom of the diagram are your left hand fingers 1, 2, and 3. The "'x" above the 6th string means don't play that particular string as you play the chord.

Place your 1st finger on the 4th string in the 2nd fret.

Place your 2nd finger on the 3rd string in the 2nd fret.

Place your 3rd finger on the 2nd string in the 2nd fret.

Hold the chord with your fingers curved and angled, press firmly but not too hard. The 1st string should sound open (no fingers touching it).

Note: Notice how all the fingers are in a straight line, directly underneath each other. Try and form a mental picture of each new chord you learn, its particular finger order and shape, that is what it looks like in your "mind's eye." Another great way to help you remember chords is to draw a guitar diagram of it yourself with horizontal lines as frets and vertical lines as strings. If you do this for each new chord you learn your recall will be much better.

Hold the "A" chord and only strum down at first. Strum smoothly and evenly. When you strum guitar chords in an exercise or song you use what's called a strum pattern, some down strokes and some up strokes. You strum a down stroke differently than you do an up stroke. When you strum a down stroke you strum completely. When you strum an up stroke you strum up and away, being careful not to strum or hit all the strings. The idea is to just hit the first few strings. Don't paintbrush the strings; strum and pull away.

Strum Pattern #1

Strum pattern #1 is called: "Down, down, up, up, down".

The best way to learn a strum pattern is to say it first. Say "Down, down, up, up, down". You might even try singing or saying it in rhythm, "Down, down, up,-up, down". There should be a very slight pause between the first up stroke and the last up stroke, about the time that it takes for you to have added another down stroke between them. The symbol for the down stroke is a lower case "n". The symbol for the up stroke is a lower case "v".

Hold the "A" chord and play "nnv-vn". Be careful not to hit the 6th string. The "x" above the 6th string means don't play that string. When you play the "A" chord, only strum 5 strings.

Strum: nnv-vn per chord

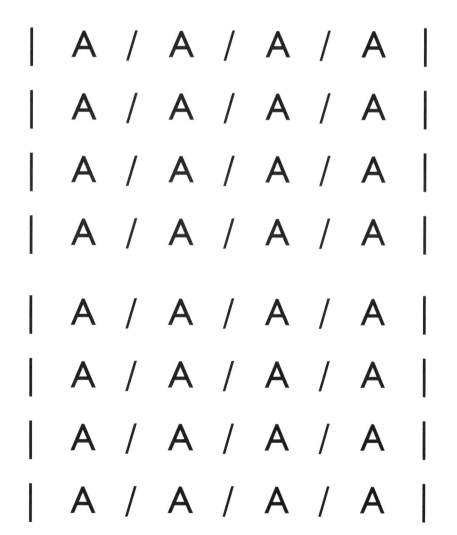

Since you've learned the "A" chord, the next two chords to learn are the "D" and the "E" chord.

_____ 🕐 10:00

The "D" Major Chord

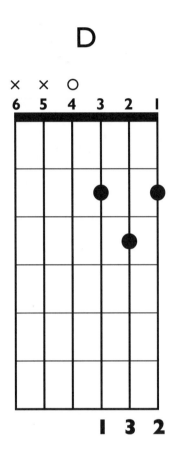

Place your 1st finger on the 3rd string in the 2nd fret.

Place your 2nd finger on the 1st string in the 2nd fret.

Place your 3rd finger on the 2nd string in the 3rd fret.

Picture the chord in your mind as a shape. Notice how the fingers are curved. It is important that you hold the chord in such a way that each finger does not slightly touch the string below the actual string you want to play.

Hold the "D" chord and strum: nnv-vn

Note: When you play the "D" chord you only strum 4 strings on the down stroke. Remember don't strike the 5th or 6th string.

The "E" Major Chord

E

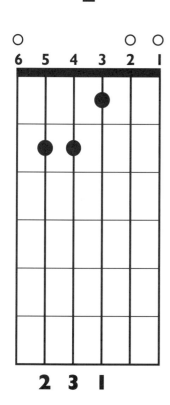

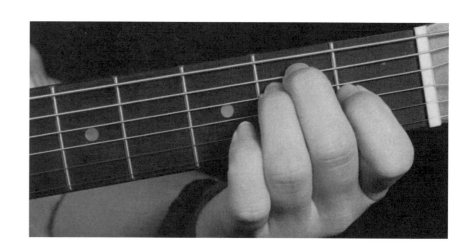

Place your 1st finger on the 3rd string in the 1st fret.

Place your 2nd finger on the 5th string in the 2nd fret.

Place your 3rd finger on the 4th string in the 2nd fret.

Picture the chord in your mind as a shape. Notice how the fingers are curved. It is important that you hold the chord in such a way that each finger does not slightly touch the string below the actual string you want to play.

Hold the "E" chord and strum: nnv-vn

Note: When you play the "E" chord you can strum all six strings on the down stroke.

_____ 11:23

CHORD PROGRESSIONS

The Three Chords in the Key of "A"

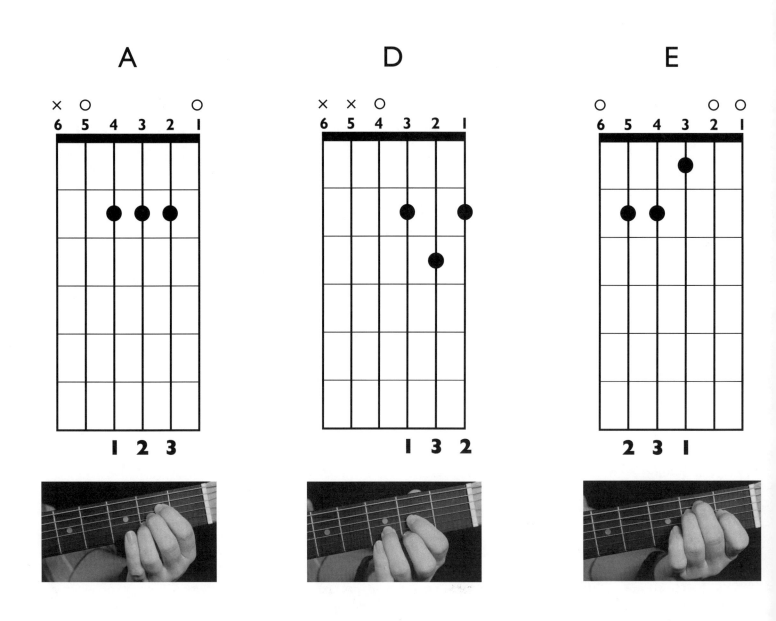

The "A", "D", and "E" chords are often played together in what is called a chord progression. A chord progression is a group of chords played in a certain order. Songs are played using chord progressions. When you play a song, you play in what is called a key. In the key of "A", the "A", "D", and "E" chords work well together. Try playing these chords in a chord progression.

Start on the "A" chord and follow with a "D" chord and then an "E" chord. Strum the pattern "nnv-vn" twice for each chord.

Note: Remember practice slowly, with a steady, even pace. Sing the strum pattern to yourself before you play.

THE THREE STEPS TO LEARNING HOW TO CHANGE CHORDS FASTER

If at this time you are having trouble changing chords quickly follow this three step method to help build your "chord changing" speed.

1. Memorize each chord by name, its shape (the way it looks and feels) and by where it is located on the fretboard.

2. Practice making and changing chords without strumming. This helps it become an automatic response so you don't hesitate between chords.

3. Strum a constant down stroke. Strum slowly at an even pace without stopping between chords. Keep strumming even when you feel like stopping to fix a chord. This forces your left hand to respond more quickly and helps you change your chords faster. At this point don't be a perfectionist about the sound of your chords; you're only trying to build up your chord changing speed.

Apply these three steps to the chords you just learned to build your chord changing speed.

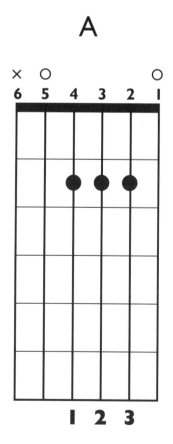

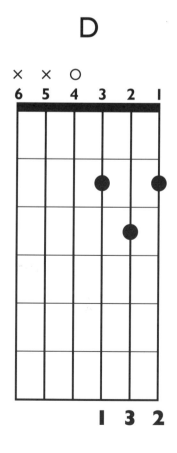

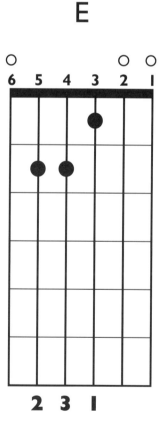

_____ 🕐 13:32

The "G" Major Chord

G

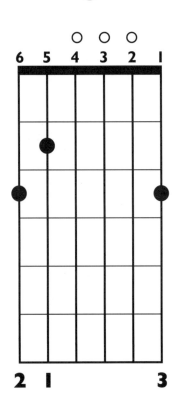

Place your 1st finger on the 5th string in the 2nd fret.

Place your 2nd finger on the 6st string in the 3rd fret.

Place your 3rd finger on the 1st string in the 3rd fret.

Picture the chord in your mind as a shape. Notice how the fingers are curved. It is important that you hold the chord in such a way that each finger does not slightly touch the string below the actual string you want to play.

Hold the "G" chord and strum: nnv-vn

repeat: nnv-vn

Note: When you play the "G" chord you can strum all 6 strings on the down stroke.

The "C" Major Chord

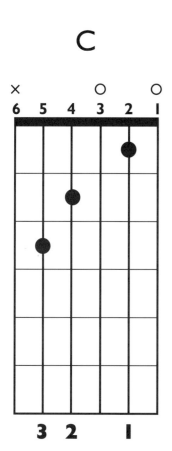

Place your 1st finger on the 2nd string in the 1st fret.

Place your 2nd finger on the 4th string in the 2nd fret.

Place your 3rd finger on the 5th string in the 3rd fret.

Picture the chord in your mind as a shape. Notice how the fingers are curved. It is important that you hold the chord in such a way that each finger does not touch the string below the actual string you want to play.

Hold the "C" chord and strum: nnv-vn

repeat: nnv-vn

Note: When you play the "C" chord, strum only five strings on the down stroke. The "x" above the 6th string means don't play that string.

_____ 🕐 14:54

The Three Chords in the Key of "G"

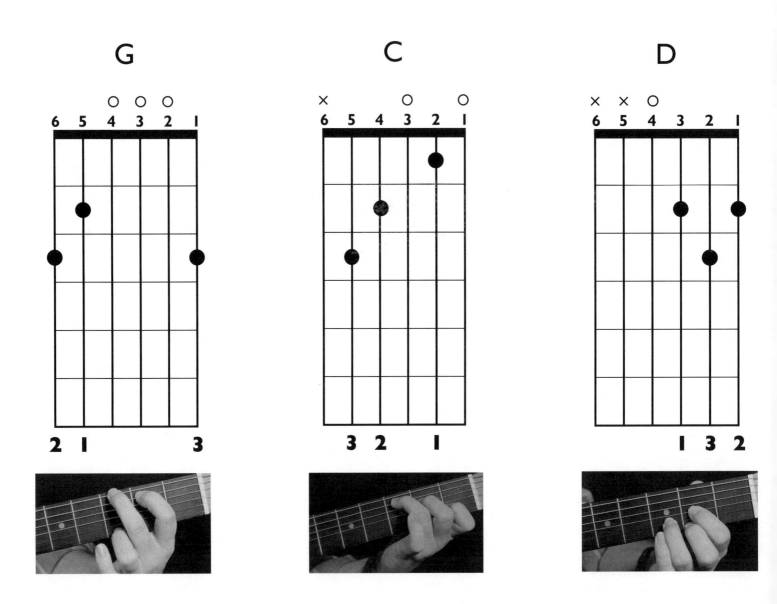

The "G", "C", and "D" chords are often played together in a chord progression. In the key of "G", the "G", "C", and "D" chords work well together. Try playing these chords together in a chord progression.

Start on the "G" chord and follow with a "C" chord and then a "D" chord. Strum the pattern "nnv-vn" twice for each chord.

Note: Remember practice slowly, with a steady, even pace. Sing or say the strum pattern to yourself before you play.

The Three Chords in the Key of "D"

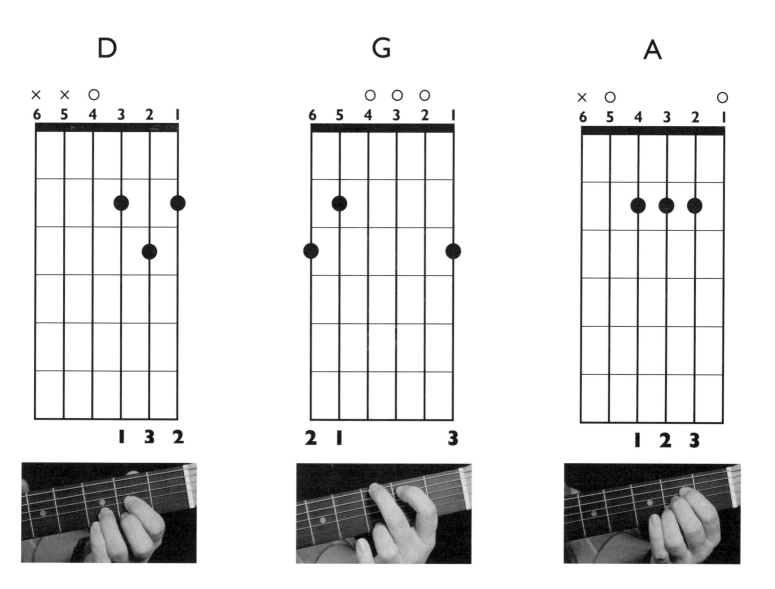

The "D", "G", and "A" chords are often played together in a chord progression. In the key of "D", the "D", "G", and "A" chords sound good together. These are chords you've already learned in a new order or chord progression.

Start on the "D" chord and follow with a "G" chord and then an "A" chord. Strum the pattern "nnv-vn" twice for each chord.

_____ 🕐 16:24

Until now you've learned only major chords. There is another kind of chord called the "minor" chord. The sound quality of the minor chord is different from the major chord. You'll notice the moody, or sad, feeling the minor chords have.

The "A" minor Chord (Am)

Am

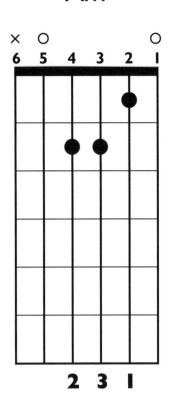

Place your 1st finger on the 2nd string in the 1st fret.

Place your 2nd finger on the 4th string in the 2nd fret.

Place your 3rd finger on the 3rd string in the 2nd fret.

The small "m" after the letter name of the chord stands for "minor" (Am = A minor).

Picture the chord in your mind as a shape. Notice how the fingers are curved. It is important that you hold the chord in such a way that each finger does not touch the string below the actual string you want to play.

Hold the "Am" chord and strum: nnv-vn

repeat: nnv-vn

Note: When you play the "Am" chord, strum only 5 strings on the down stroke. The "x" above the 6th string means don't play that string.

The "E" minor Chord (Em)

Em

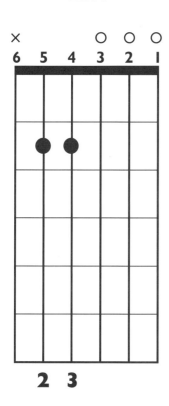

Place your 2nd finger on the 5th string in the 2nd fret.

Place your 3rd finger on the 4th string in the 2nd fret.

Picture the chord in your mind as a shape. Notice how the fingers are curved.

Hold the "Em" chord and strum: nnv-vn

repeat: nnv-vn

Note: When you play the "Em" chord you can strum all 6 strings on the down stroke.

⏱ 19:06

The "D" minor Chord (Dm)

Dm

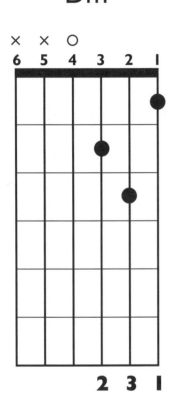

Place your 1st finger on the 1st string in the 1st fret.

Place your 2nd finger on the 3rd string in the 2nd fret.

Place your 3rd finger on the 2nd string in the 3rd fret.

Picture the chord in your mind as a shape. Notice how the fingers are curved.

Hold the "Dm" chord and strum: nnv-vn

repeat: nnv-vn

*Note: When you play the "Dm" chord you strum 4 strings on the down stroke.

The "F#" minor Chord (F#m)

F#m

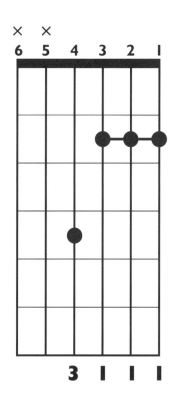

Place your 1st finger across the 1st 3 strings in the second fret. Using your index finger like a "bar" hold down all 3 strings.

Place your 3rd finger on the 4th string in the 4th fret.

Picture the chord in your mind as a shape. Be careful not to let your 3rd finger overlap and touch string 1, 2, or 3. Hold the "F#m" chord and strum: nnv-vn

repeat: nnv-vn

*Note: The symbol "#" in music means sharp.

*Note: When you play the "F#m" chord you strum 4 strings on the down stroke.

*Note: The thumb is very important in this chord and can be used behind the neck to support the bar position.

_____ ⏱ 20:03

The "F" Major Chord

F

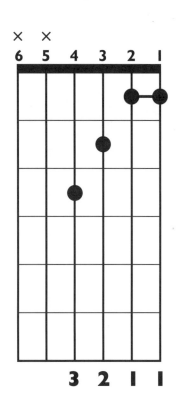

Place your 1st finger over both string 1 and 2 using a bar position in the 1st fret.

Place your 2nd finger on the 3rd string in the 2nd fret.

Place your 3rd finger on the 4th string in the 3rd fret.

Picture the chord in your mind as a shape. Be careful not to let your 2nd or 3rd finger overlap and touch any other strings.

Hold the "F" chord and strum: nnv-vn

repeat: nnv-vn

*Note: When you play the "F" chord, strum 4 strings on the down stroke.

*Note: The thumb is very important in this chord and can be used behind the neck to support the bar position.

CHORD REVIEW PAGE

These are the diagrams for all of the chords you've learned.

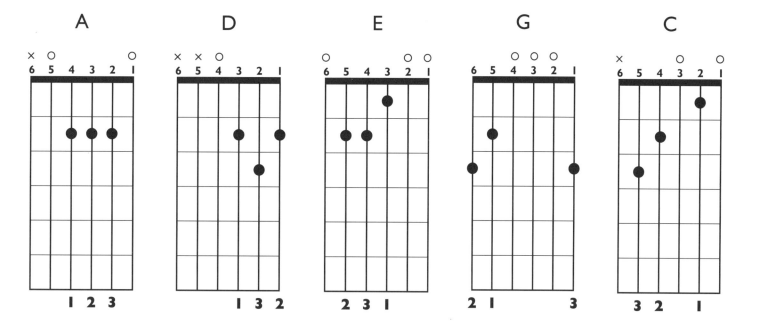

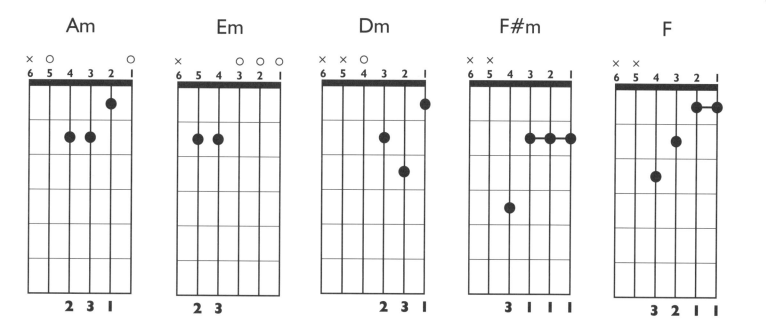

21:27

CHORD PROGRESSION PRACTICE

The next section of the book is designed for your own personal practice, and to use all of the chords, skills, and techniques you've learned. Chord diagrams used in each chord progression are shown below. The first exercise song uses four of the chords you've learned: "G", "Em", "C", and "D". The strum pattern is down, down, up, up, down, (nnv-vn). You are playing the rhythm accompaniment to the melody. Each space divided by diagonal lines is called a measure.

Chord Progression #1

This chord progression is a rhythm accompaniment in the style of "Stand by Me".

G

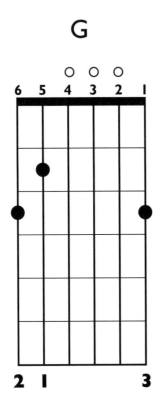

Em

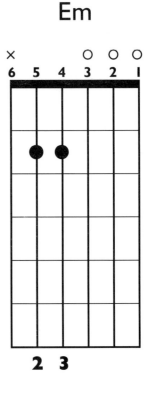

C

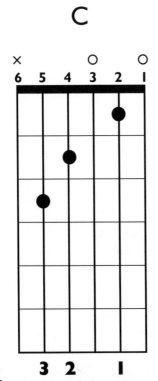

D

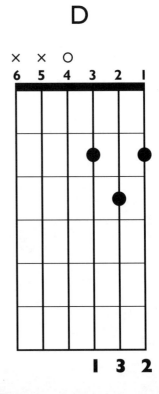

Strum: nnv-vn per measure, or per chord.
Count to yourself or out loud before you start playing: 1,2,3 play

| G / G / Em / Em / C / D / G / G |

| G / G / Em / Em / C / D / G / G |

| G / G / Em / Em / C / D / G / G |

| G / G / Em / Em / C / D / G / G |

| G / G / Em / Em / C / D / G / G |

| G / G / Em / Em / C / D / G / G |

| G / G / Em / Em / C / D / G / G |

| G / G / Em / Em / C / D / G / G |

*Note: A recorded version of this chord progression can be found in the video songbook section of "Learn Guitar on VCR" volume 1.

Chord Progression #2

This chord progression is a rhythm accompaniment in the style of "House of the Rising Sun".

The second exercise song uses the chords "Am", "C", "D", "F", and "E". In this song you pick out the notes instead of strumming as before. Use a new pattern called: bass, brush, pick. Pick out the bass note of each chord, brush down from that bass note, then pick up the first three notes of each chord.

The bass note that you pick out for the "Am" chord is the 5th string played open. Brush down, and pick up the first three notes of the chord (string 1, 2, and 3).

The bass note that you pick out for the "C" chord is the 5th string you are holding as you play the "C" chord. Brush down, and pick up the first three notes of the chord (string 1, 2, and 3).

The bass note that you pick out for the "D" chord is the fourth string played open. Brush down, and pick up the first three notes of the chord (string 1, 2, and 3).

The bass note that you pick out for the "F" chord is the fourth string you are holding as you play the "F" chord. Brush down, and pick up the first three notes of the chord (string 1, 2, and 3).

The bass note that you pick out for the "E" chord is the 6th string played open. Brush down, and pick up the first three notes of the chord (string 1, 2, and 3).

The bass note of each chord is indicated by the number above the chord diagram.

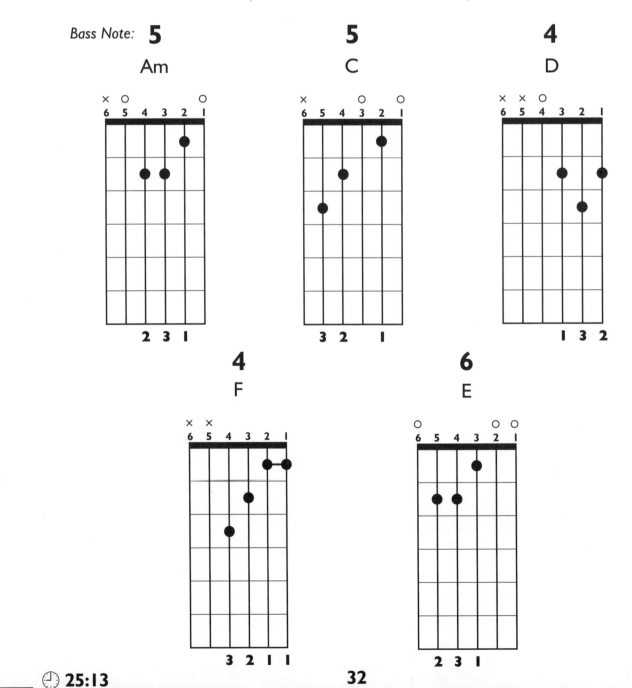

Pick/strum pattern: Bass, brush, pick=per chord

| Am / C / D / F |

| Am / C / E / E |

| Am / C / D / F |

| Am / E / Am / E |

| Am / C / D / F |

| Am / C / E / E |

| Am / C / D / F |

| Am / E / Am / E / Am |

Note: A recorded version of this chord progression can be found in the video songbook section of "Learn Guitar on VCR" volume 1.

Chord Progression #3

This chord progression is a rhythm accompaniment in the style of "Oh Pretty Woman".

The third exercise song uses all the chords learned in the book. It starts with a simple melody introduction of single notes. Use a down, up stroke to pick out the single notes in the introduction. Assign your 1st finger to the 2nd fret, your 2nd finger to the 3rd fret, your 3rd finger to the 4th fret, and your 4th finger to the 5th fret. This is called playing in second position. The first part of the song has been notated using "string/fret" tablature, first number string, second number fret.

6/0 would be the 6th string played open. Play it twice.
6/4 would be the 6th string 4th fret.
5/2 would be the 5th string 2nd fret.
5/5 would be the 5th string 5th fret with your little finger.

Note: During the rhythm accompaniment strum: nnv-vn for each chord.

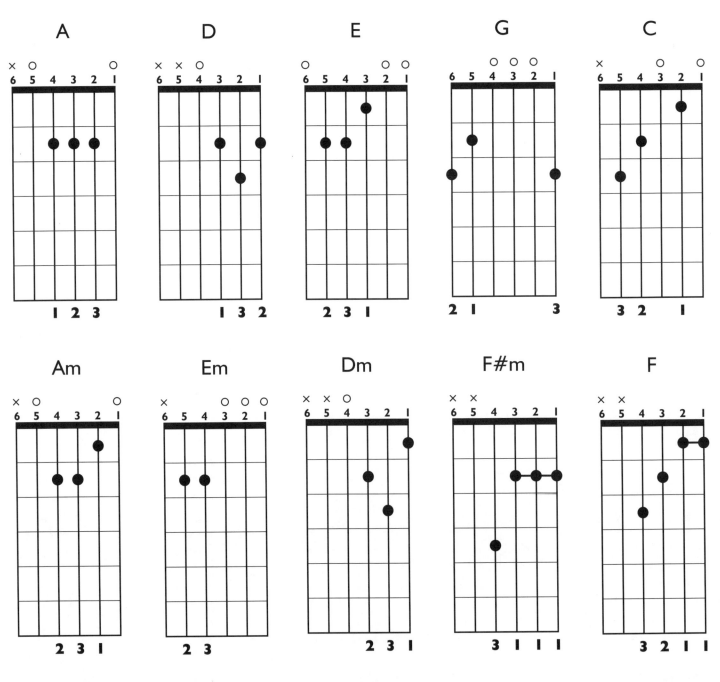

||:=repeat sign, repeats what's between.... :||
Use "nv" stroke for all single notes, and solo.
Start by counting 1,2,3,4

string/fret

||: 6/0 6/0 6/4 5/2 5/5 :|| play this line two times

rest, count 1,2,3,4, 1,2,3,4. play again...

solo line: string/fret

||:6/0 6/0 6/4 5/2 5/5 4/4 4/2 5/5 :|| play this line four times

strum pattern: nnv-vn per measure

| A / F#m / A / F#m / D / D / E / E / E / E |

solo line: string/fret

||:6/0 6/0 6/4 5/2 5/5 4/4 4/2 5/5 :|| play this line four times

strum pattern: nnv-vn per measure

| A / F#m / A / F#m / D / D / E / E / E / E |

solo line: string/fret

||:6/0 6/0 6/4 5/2 5/5 4/4 4/2 5/5 :|| play this line four times

rhythm: nnv-vn per measure

|Dm / G / C / Am / F / G / C / A |

|Dm / G / C / Am / F / G / C / A |

strum pattern: nnv-vn per measure

| D / D / E / E |

| A / F#m / D / E / E / E / E |

solo line: string/fret

||:6/0 6/0 6/4 5/2 5/5 4/4 4/2 5/5 :|| play this line eight times (fade out).

Note: A recorded version of this chord progression can be found in the video songbook section of "Learn Guitar on VCR" volume 1.

BLANK CHORD DIAGRAM PAGE

BLANK CHORD DIAGRAM PAGE

Blank chord diagrams are included for you to draw the chords you've learned. Drawing each chord yourself will help you to remember them.

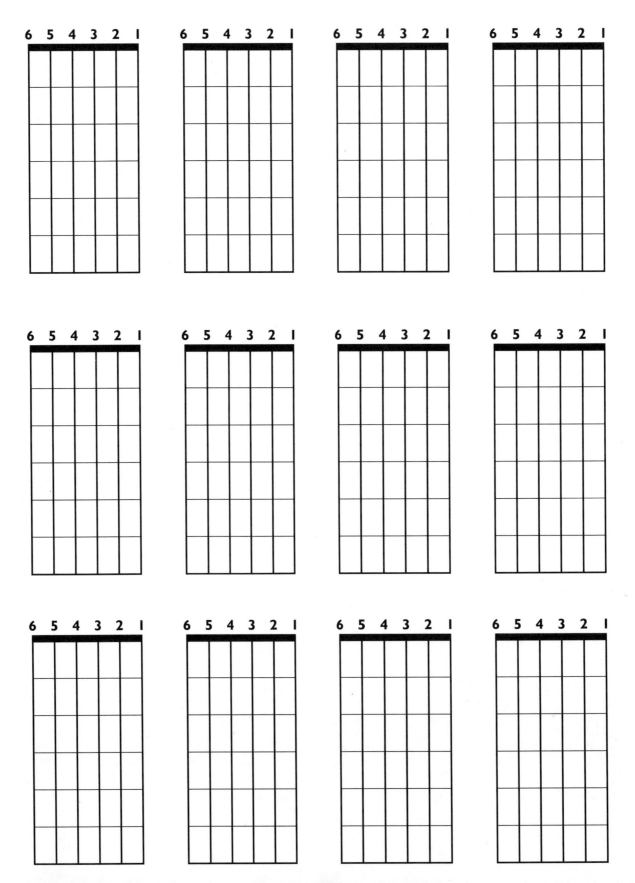